WITCHES' BREW

and Other HORRIFYING PARTY FOODS

Ali Vega

Lerner Publications ◆ Minneapolis

Lerner Publications Company
A division of Lerner Publishing Group, Inc.
241 First Avenue North
Minneapolis, MN 55401 USA

For reading levels and more information, look up this title at www.lernerbooks.com.

Main body text set in Tw Cen MT Std.
Typeface provided by Monotype.

Library of Congress Cataloging-in-Publication Data

Names: Vega, Ali, author.
Title: Witches' brew and other horrifying party foods / by Ali Vega.
Description: Minneapolis : Lerner Publications, [2017] | Series: Little kitchen of horrors |
Audience: Ages 7-11. | Audience: Grades 4 to 6. | Includes bibliographical references and
index.
Identifiers: LCCN 2016020549 (print) | LCCN 2016021944 (ebook) | ISBN 9781512425765 (lb
: alk. paper) | ISBN 9781512428087 (eb pdf)
Subjects: LCSH: Holiday cooking--Juvenile literature. | Children's parties--Juvenile
literature. | Cooking--Juvenile literature. | Halloween cooking--Juvenile literature. | LCGFT:
Cookbooks.
Classification: LCC TX739.2.H34 V44 2017 (print) | LCC TX739.2.H34 (ebook) | DDC
641.5/68--dc23

LC record available at https://lccn.loc.gov/2016020549

Manufactured in the United States of America
1-41344-23288-8/31/2016

Photo Acknowledgments
The images in this book are used with the permission of: © Jason Lugo/iStockphoto, p. 4;
© Mighty Media, Inc., pp. 5 (top left), 5 (top right), 5 (bottom), 9 (left), 9 (right), 10, 11 (top),
11 (bottom), 12, 13 (top), 13 (middle), 13 (bottom), 14, 15 (top), 15 (middle), 15 (bottom),
16, 17 (top), 17 (middle), 17 (bottom), 18, 19 (top), 19 (middle), 19 (bottom), 20, 21 (top), 21
(middle), 21 (bottom), 22, 23 (top), 23 (middle), 23 (bottom), 24, 25 (top), 25 (middle), 25
(bottom), 27 (top), 27 (middle), 27 (bottom), 28, 29 (top), 29 (bottom); © Elena Elisseeva/
Shutterstock Images, p. 6; © darkscott/iStockphoto, p. 7; © Szepy/Thinkstock, p. 8;
© Ronnachai Palas/Shutterstock Images, p. 30.

Front Cover: © Mighty Media, Inc.

CONTENTS

Introduction: Foul Party Foods   4

Before You Get Started   6

Puke-Worthy Party Treats   8

Earwax on a Stick   10

Shrunken-Head Punch   12

Stabbed Eyeballs   14

Weenie Witch Fingers   16

Witches' Brew   18

Dog-Pile Treats   20

Black Widow Cheese Ball   22

Monster Boogers   24

Crispy Mice   26

Wrapping Up   30

Glossary   31

Further Information   31

Index   32

Introduction
FOUL PARTY FOODS

Imagine you're at a party and scoping out the snack table. You'd probably expect to find fruity punch, crunchy snacks, and towers of treats. But what if there were shrunken heads bobbing in the punch? Or blobs of brown butterscotch earwax clinging to pretzel sticks? Picture a plate of chocolate cookies labeled "dog doo-doo." These snacks may seem disgusting. But you'd be in for a tasty surprise!

Revolting party foods are tons of fun to make and serve. Their sick-sounding names and appearances are just a trick. These dishes actually taste delicious! You will happily horrify your guests with party foods that look and sound gross. So put on your apron and party hat, and start making some foul eats fit for any fiesta!

Before You
GeT STaRTeD

Cook Safely! Creating horrifying party foods means using different kitchen tools and appliances. These items can be very hot or sharp. Make sure to get an adult's help whenever making a recipe that requires use of an oven, stove, or knife.

Be a Smart Chef! Cooking terrifying party foods can be messy. Ask an adult for permission before starting a new cooking project. Then make sure you have a clean workspace. Wash your hands often while cooking. If you have long hair, be sure to tie it back. Make sure your guests don't have any food allergies before cooking. Adjust the recipes if you need to. Make sure your petrifying party foods are safe to eat!

Tools You'll Need

Cooking can involve special tools and appliances. You will need the following items for these disgusting recipes:

- food processor or blender
- freezer
- microwave
- oven
- refrigerator

METRIC CONVERSION CHART

Use this handy chart to convert recipes to the metric system. If you can't find the conversion you need, ask an adult to help you find an online calculator!

STANDARD	METRIC
¼ teaspoon	1.2 milliliters
½ teaspoon	2.5 ml
¾ teaspoon	3.7 ml
1 teaspoon	5 ml
2 teaspoons	10 ml
1 tablespoon	15 ml
¼ cup	59 ml
⅓ cup	79 ml
½ cup	118 ml
⅔ cup	158 ml
¾ cup	177 ml
1 cup	237 ml

150 degrees Fahrenheit	66 degrees Celsius
300°F	149°C
350°F	177°C
400°F	204°C

1 ounce	28 grams
1 fluid ounce	30 milliliters
1 inch	2.5 centimeters
1 pound	0.5 kilograms

PUKE-WORTHY PARTY TREATS

Disgusting Titles

A nasty name makes any party food even more disgusting! Cocktail weenies become cut-off fingers. Creamy butterscotch looks like oozing earwax. And glazed popcorn turns into crusty monster boogers!

As you cook, get creative! Do any ingredients inspire you to call them by nasty names? Share the disgusting title of each party dish you serve with your guests. Their looks of horror are part of the fun!

Appalling Party Props

It takes more than nauseating names to make party foods truly petrifying. The way you present these sickening dishes is also important. Find fun props to play up the grossness of each dish. A fake severed hand is the perfect prop for cocktail-weenie fingers. Plastic bugs, bandages, toilet paper, and other items help keep your party foods extra creepy. Make sure you **sanitize** any props before using them. And remove any non-**edible** props before serving your party foods to guests. Keep things fun and delicious without putting your diners in danger.

EARWAX ON A STICK

Partygoers won't know whether to lick their lips or clean their ears when they see these crusty treats!

Ingredients

40–60 mini marshmallows (1 bag)
20–30 pretzel sticks
½ cup butterscotch chips

Tools

- baking sheet
- waxed paper
- microwave-safe bowl
- measuring cups
- mixing spoon

**Serves: 10–15
Preparation Time:
30–45 minutes**

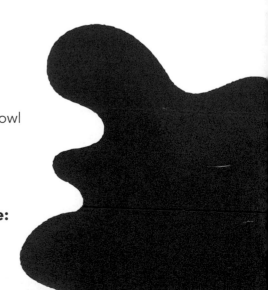

1. Cover a baking sheet with waxed paper. Push a mini marshmallow onto each end of the pretzel sticks.

2. Put the butterscotch chips in a bowl. Microwave them for 30 seconds on high. Stir to see if the chips are melted. If not, heat the chips for another 30 seconds and stir again. Repeat until the chips are fully melted.

3. Dip the marshmallow on one end of a pretzel stick into the melted butterscotch. Then dip the other end. Place the stick on the baking sheet to cool.

4. Repeat step 3 with the remaining sticks. Now see if your guests can stomach these sweet chunks of ear gunk!

TIP

For an extra-sweet treat, add a mini chocolate chip to the end of each marshmallow after dipping it in butterscotch.

SHRUNKEN-HEAD PUNCH

Carve crisp apples into tiny bobbing
heads that grimace at guests.

Ingredients

2 cups lemon juice
2 tablespoons coarse salt
8–10 Granny Smith apples
10 cups apple juice
2 cups cranberry juice
3 cups orange juice
3 cups club soda

Tools

• baking sheet
• parchment paper
• medium mixing bowl
• measuring cups
• measuring spoons
• mixing spoon
• peeler
• knife
• cutting board
• plate
• dish towel or paper towel
• oven mitts
• large punch bowl

Serves: 15
Preparation Time: 3 hours

1. **Preheat** the oven to 250°F. Cover a baking sheet with parchment paper. In a medium bowl, stir together the lemon juice and salt.

2. Peel the apples, and cut each one in half. Remove the cores and seeds. With an adult's help, carefully carve a face in the apple.

3. Cover a plate with a dish towel or paper towel. Put each apple facedown in the lemon and salt mixture for 1 minute. Remove and set each apple facedown on the plate to drain.

3

4. Place the apples face up on the baking sheet, and bake for 90 to 115 minutes, or until the edges begin to brown. Remove the apples from the oven, and let them cool completely.

5. Pour the apple juice, cranberry juice, orange juice, and club soda into a large punch bowl, and stir together.

4

6. Drop the apple heads into the punch so they glare at your guests!

STABBED EYEBALLS

Freshly-plucked fruit eyeballs stare at you from the other side of a toothpick.

Serves: 10–20
Preparation Time:
30–45 minutes

Ingredients

honeydew melon
½ cup strawberry jam
30–40 blueberries

Tools

- knife
- cutting board
- spoon
- melon baller
- table knife
- measuring cups
- measuring spoons
- 30–40 toothpicks
- serving platter

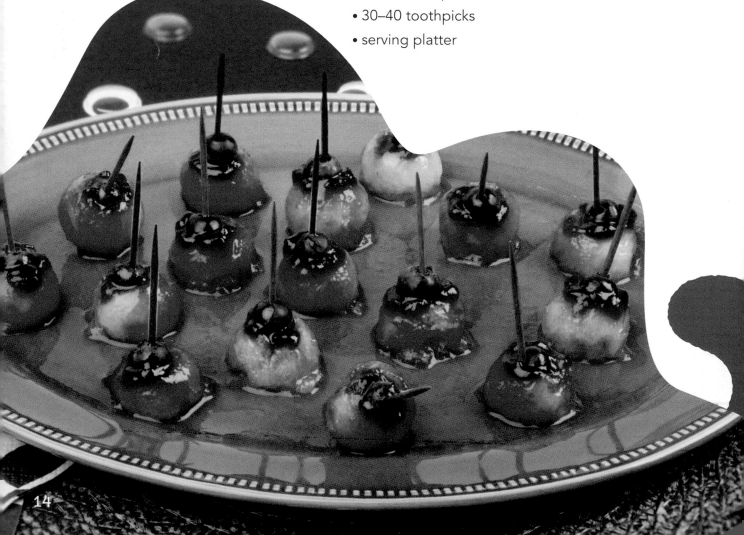

1. With an adult's help, cut the honeydew melon in half. Scoop out the seeds with a spoon. Use the melon baller to scoop out 30 to 40 melon balls. These will be the eyeballs.

2. Gently carve a hole in the middle of each melon ball using a table knife.

3. Put about ¼ teaspoon of jam in each melon ball's hole.

4. Place a blueberry on top of the jam in each melon ball.

5. Stick a toothpick in each eyeball for serving.

6. Arrange the eyeballs on a platter, and watch your guests pick up these fruity peepers.

TIP

If blueberries are not in season where you live, try using raisins instead.

WEENIE WITCH FINGERS

Wrinkled weenie fingers look like they came from a witch's wiggling hand!

Serves: 10–20
Preparation Time: 1 hour

Ingredients

1 14-ounce package mini cocktail
　　wieners
1 white onion
½ cup ketchup

Tools

- medium saucepan
- cutting board
- knife
- colander
- measuring cups
- measuring spoons
- serving plate

1. Fill a medium saucepan three-quarters full with water. With an adult's help, bring the water to a **boil** over high heat. Lay the weenies out on a cutting board. Carefully cut a notch out of the tip of each weenie.

2. Cut shallow slits in the weenies to look like knuckles. Look at your own fingers for inspiration!

3. Cut the onion into thick slices. Each should be about ¾ inch wide and 1 inch long. You will need one slice for each weenie. Put the onion slices and weenies in the boiling water. Cook the weenies according to the package directions.

4. With an adult's help, drain the weenies and onion slices using a colander. Let them cool.

5. Transfer the weenies to a clean surface. Spread about ¼ teaspoon of ketchup in each weenie's notch. Place an onion slice on top of the ketchup to look like a fingernail.

6. Arrange the fingers on a serving plate, and spread the rest of the ketchup around to look like blood. Your guests won't be able to keep their hands off these fingers!

1

2

5

TIP

For more festive fingernails, try slices of green, yellow, or orange peppers.

WITCHES' BREW

This creepy cauldron will make party guests cackle with delight.

Serves: 10–20
Preparation Time: 25 hours (1 hour active)

Ingredients

4 cups cranberry juice

5 cups pineapple juice

1 12-ounce can frozen lemonade, thawed

½ cup lemon juice

1 bunch green grapes

8 cups ginger ale

Tools

- 2 disposable gloves
- measuring cups
- 2 rubber bands
- shallow baking dish
- punch bowl
- long-handled spoon
- kitchen scissors
- knife

cutting board

1. Wash the gloves with soap and water.

2. Carefully pour about 1½ cups of cranberry juice into each glove. Fill the gloves just past the wrist, and secure each with a rubber band. Place both gloves in a baking dish, and freeze for 24 hours.

2

3. Pour the remaining cranberry juice and the pineapple juice, lemonade, and lemon juice into a large punch bowl. Stir together.

4. Take your frozen gloves out of the freezer. Carefully cut a large slit in the palm of each glove. Gently peel the glove off the frozen hand. Be extra careful around the fingers!

4

5. Rinse the grapes, and slice each one in half. Add the grapes and ginger ale to the punch. Serve to your guests, and warn them to watch out for slimy eyeballs!

5

TIP

Many people have latex allergies, so make sure your gloves are latex-free!

DOG-PILE TREATS

Create cocoa cookies that look just like poo piles from the lawn!

Ingredients

½ cup peanut butter
¼ cup cocoa powder
1 cup milk
2 teaspoons vanilla extract
½ cup oatmeal
¾ cup brown sugar
2½ cups flour, plus extra for coating your hands
¼ cup raisins or chocolate chips
¼ cup raw sunflower seeds

Serves: 10–20
Preparation Time: 1 hour

Tools

• 2 baking sheets
• parchment paper
• measuring cups
• measuring spoons
• large mixing bowl
• mixing spoon
• oven mitts
• wire cooling rack

1 Preheat the oven to 325°F. Cover two baking sheets with parchment paper.

2 Put all the ingredients in a mixing bowl and stir together.

3 Coat your clean hands with flour. Then roll a ball of dough about the size of a golf ball.

4 Roll and stretch the ball into a poo shape, and place it on a baking sheet.

5 Repeat steps 3 and 4 until all the dough is used. Combine some dough chunks to form piles.

6 Bake the cookies for 20 to 25 minutes, Remove the cookies from the oven, and let them cool on a wire rack. No pooper-scooper needed for these tasty poo piles!

BLACK WIDOW CHEESE BALL

Use crackers to scoop up the creamy cheese guts of a supersized spider.

Serves: 10
Preparation Time: 1 hour

Ingredients

4 large shallots
3 tablespoons unsalted butter
10 ounces fresh goat cheese
10 ounces cream cheese
1 cup black sesame seeds
¼ red pepper
crackers for serving

Tools

• knife
• cutting board
• measuring spoons
• frying pan
• food processor or blender
• measuring cups
• large plate
• serving platter
• 4 black pipe cleaners
• scissors

1. Peel the shallots, and chop each one into a few small pieces. Then with an adult's help, melt the butter in a frying pan over medium-low heat. Add the shallots to the butter and **sauté** over medium heat for 8 to 10 minutes. Remove from heat and let the shallots cool.

1

2. Put the shallots, goat cheese, and cream cheese in the food processor or blender. Blend on high for 2 to 3 minutes, or until smooth. Chill in the refrigerator for 30 minutes.

3. With clean hands, roll about ⅓ of the cheese mixture into a ball. Roll the rest of the mixture into a larger ball.

2

4. Spread the sesame seeds out onto a large plate. Roll both cheese balls in the seeds until the balls are completely covered.

5. Arrange the balls side by side on a serving platter. They should look like the head and body of a spider. Cut four pipe cleaners in half. Stick four pipe cleaner pieces into each side of the body. They should be spaced evenly to look like legs.

6. Cut the red pepper into small pieces, and arrange them in a pattern on the spider's back. Serve this spooky spider with crackers to startle your guests!

4

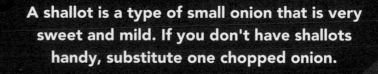

A shallot is a type of small onion that is very sweet and mild. If you don't have shallots handy, substitute one chopped onion.

MONSTER BOOGERS

Popcorn glazed in sweet sauce becomes beastly boogers coated in snot!

Serves: 10–15
Preparation Time: 30 minutes

Ingredients

12 cups popped popcorn
12 tablespoons (1½ sticks) butter
2 cups sugar
¾ cup light corn syrup
3 tablespoons vanilla extract
green food coloring
4 cups butterscotch chips

Tools

- measuring cups
- large bowl
- baking sheet
- parchment paper
- medium saucepan
- mixing spoon
- measuring spoons

1 Put the popcorn in a large bowl. Cover a baking sheet with parchment paper.

2 With an adult's help, melt the butter in the saucepan over medium-low heat. Add the sugar, and stir for 5 to 7 minutes. Then stir in the corn syrup, vanilla extract, and several drops of food coloring.

2

3 Remove the saucepan from the heat, and carefully drizzle the sweet mixture over the popcorn. Stir until coated.

4 Let the mixture cool. Then add the butterscotch chips, and mix some more.

3

5 With clean hands, form a golf ball-sized amount of the popcorn mixture into a booger-shaped lump and place on the baking sheet. Repeat until all your boogers are made. Then place the baking sheet in the freezer for 10 minutes.

6 Remove the baking sheet from the freezer, and your boogers are ready to serve! Give guests a stack of tissues to mop up any sticky drips or massive globs.

5

With an adult's help, you can pop your own popcorn by heating 3 tablespoons of olive oil in a large stockpot over medium heat. When the oil is hot, add ½ cup unpopped kernels, and put a lid on the pot. Cook for 5 to 7 minutes, shaking the pot constantly to keep the popcorn from burning. When you hear the popping stop, remove from heat. Repeat until you have enough popcorn!

25

CRISPY MICE

These stuffed rodents won't squeak once they're cooked!

Serves: 10-15
Preparation Time: 2 hours (45 minutes active)

Ingredients

1 sweet onion
1 red pepper
3 cups shredded Monterey jack cheese
20–30 spaghetti strands
2 teaspoons paprika
1 teaspoon garlic powder
6 tablespoons butter, softened
10 ounces cream cheese
1½ teaspoons salt
1 teaspoon ground pepper
10–15 Anaheim peppers (or any narrow, mild peppers)
40–60 pretzel sticks
2 cups flour
2 eggs
½ cup milk
1½ cup breadcrumbs
cooking spray

Tools

- knife
- cutting board
- mixing bowls, various sizes
- measuring cups
- medium saucepan
- colander
- measuring spoons
- mixing spoons
- **whisk**
- baking sheets
- baking pan with grilling rack
- oven mitts
- serving plate

1 Chop the onion into ¼-inch pieces. Then chop the red pepper into ½-inch pieces. Put the onion and pepper pieces in a medium bowl, and add the Monterey jack cheese.

2 With an adult's help, fill a saucepan three-quarters full with water, and bring it to a boil over medium-high heat. Then add the spaghetti, and cook for 8 to 10 minutes, or until done. Carefully drain the spaghetti with a colander, and let it cool.

3

3 Put the paprika, garlic powder, butter, cream cheese, 1 teaspoon salt, and ½ teaspoon pepper in a large bowl. Stir together. Stir in the onion, pepper, and cheese mixture. Then refrigerate for 30 to 45 minutes.

4 Cut off the Anaheim peppers' stems. Then cut each pepper in half the long way. Use a spoon to scrape the seeds off each pepper's interior. Discard the seeds.

4

5 Lay the peppers open-side up on a baking sheet. These are your mouse bodies. Place one strand of cooked spaghetti in each pepper half. Leave about 4 inches of the strand hanging out of the pepper, to look like a tail.

6 Add a few spoonfuls of the cheese filling to each pepper. Set two pretzels on top of each pepper half to look like legs. Add one more spoonful of filling to cover the pretzels' centers.

Crispy Mice continued next page

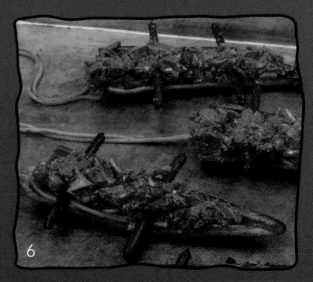
6

TIP

Serve your mice with a side of ranch dressing or hot sauce for some extra flavor.

*Crispy Mice,
continued*

7 Put 1 cup of flour in a small bowl. Whisk the eggs and milk together in a separate bowl. In a third bowl, stir together the breadcrumbs, 1 cup flour, ½ teaspoon salt, and ½ teaspoon ground pepper.

8 Coat a clean baking sheet in cooking spray. Then coat one pepper mouse in cooking spray. Carefully dip the mouse in the flour bowl, and use clean hands to coat it with flour. Next dip the mouse in the egg and milk mixture. Finally coat the mouse in the breading mixture, and set it feet-side down on a baking sheet. Repeat with the remaining mice, and refrigerate for 1 hour.

9 Preheat the oven to 375°F. Coat the grill rack with cooking spray, and place the rack in the baking pan.

10 Arrange the mice feet-side down on the grill rack. Bake for 30 to 45 minutes.

11 Remove the pan from the oven, and let it cool for 10 minutes.

12 Arrange the mice on a serving plate, and tell guests to gobble them up before they scurry away!

WRAPPING UP

Cleaning Up

Once you are done cooking, it is time to clean up! Make sure to wipe up spills, wash dishes, and clear the table. Wash and put away any props you used that don't belong in the kitchen. Make sure any leftovers are properly packaged and refrigerated.

Keep Cooking!

Let the foul party foods you made inspire you! Think of ways to put new, terrifying twists on the recipes you tried. Or dream up new ideas for gag-worthy party dishes. Think gross, and keep on cooking!

GLOSSARY

boil: liquid that has become so hot that bubbles form and rise to the top

edible: something that can be safely eaten

latex: a substance used to make some rubber products

preheat: to heat an oven to the required temperature before putting in the food

sanitize: to clean something so it is free of germs

sauté: to fry in a bit of butter or oil

whisk: to stir very quickly using a fork or a tool made of curved wire, also called a whisk

FURTHER INFORMATION

Cook, Deanna F. *Cooking Class: 57 Fun Recipes Kids Will Love to Make (and Eat)!* North Adams, MA: Storey Publishing, 2015. Learn helpful cooking tips and tricks to get started in the kitchen.

Cornell, Kari A. *Sweet Cookies and Bars.* Minneapolis: Millbrook Press, 2014. The sweet treats in this book make the perfect party foods.

Kid Chef Recipes
http://allrecipes.com/recipes/15096/everyday-cooking/family-friendly/kid-chefs/
Put your own spooky twist on these fun and easy recipes for your next party!

29 Spooktacular Halloween Recipes
https://www.babble.com/best-recipes/halloween-recipes-kids-treats-party-food
These creepy foods are sure to make your next spooky celebration a hit!

INDEX

adult help, 6, 7, 13, 15, 17, 23, 25, 27

allergies, 6, 19

black widow cheese ball, 22–23

cleaning up, 30

crispy mice, 26–29

dog-pile treats, 4, 20–21

earwax on a stick, 4, 8, 10–11

getting started, 4–9

ingredients, 8, 10, 12, 14, 16, 18, 20–21, 22, 24, 26

metric conversion chart, 7

monster boogers, 8, 24–25

names, 5, 8–9

presentation, 9

props, 9, 30

safety, 6

shrunken-head punch, 4, 12–13

stabbed eyeballs, 14–15

tools, 6, 10, 12, 14, 16, 18, 20, 22, 24, 26

weenie witch fingers, 16–17

witches' brew, 18–19